Hebrew Holiday and Folk Songs
22 well-known Hebrew

with lyrics, translations and guitar chords
Compiled and arranged by Renee and David Karp

These songs and dances represent a cross-section of some of the best-known Hebrew music, ranging from liturgical and folk (including one Yiddish song) to the festive holidays of Chanuka, Purim, and Passover. Happiness and sorrow, moments of hardship and moments of tenderness are all expressed through the songs in this collection.

Arranged especially for upper elementary to lower intermediate pianists, these arrangements may be enjoyed by anyone desiring to explore Hebrew music. The keys have been selected based on their suitability of singing range and pianistic comfort. It is our hope that your enjoyment in playing and singing these songs will equal ours in having prepared them.

Renee and David Karp

Pronunciation Guide

Every language has its special sounds. Below is a guide to help you in pronouncing the Hebrew words in this book.

a	as in *mama*
e	as in *bet*
eh	as in *bet,* used only at the end of the word
i	as in *sit* or *thing*
o	as in *softer* or *some* and sometimes long o as in *home*
u	as in *bull* or *mule*
oi	as in *foil*
ei	as in *veil*
g	as in *got* (hard *g*)
ch	as in *Bach*

Editor: Carole Flatau
Cover Design: Joann Carrera

Contents

Contents by Category

for advanced arrangements of these songs plus 12 additional pieces, see **Chanukah, Folk and Festivals**, EL9545

Chanukah

Chanukah is observed for eight days and is sometimes called the Festival of Lights. This holiday celebrates religious freedom.

During each of the eight nights, the candles on the menorah are kindled and prayers are said. Following this ritual, songs are sung, games are played and potato latkes (pancakes) and jelly donuts are eaten.

O' Chanukah, O' Chanuka

Rock of Ages

My Dreidel

Chanukah

O' CHANUKAH, O' CHANUKAH

*Lighting the menorah, eating latkes and playing with dreidels -
all are wonderful rituals of the Chanukah festival.*

TRADITIONAL
Arranged by DAVID KARP

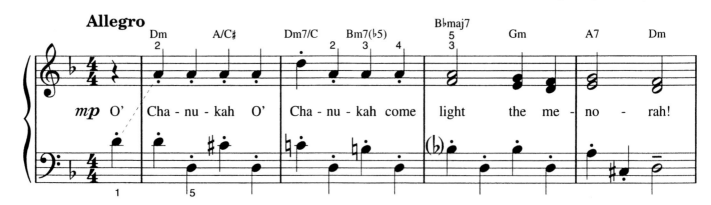

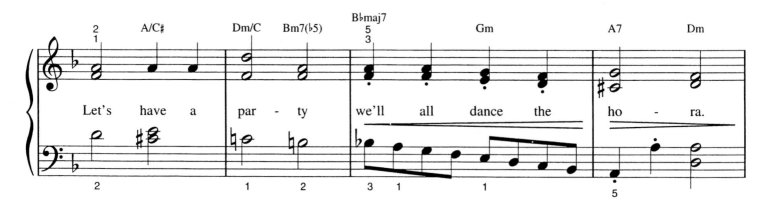

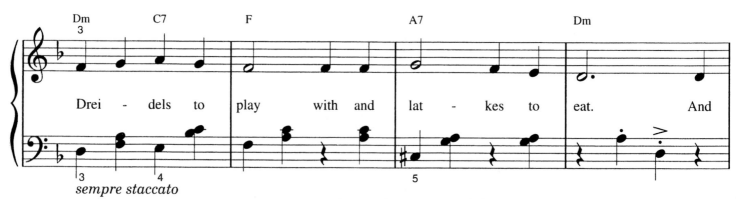

sempre staccato

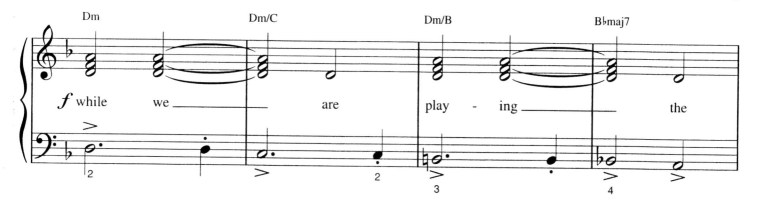

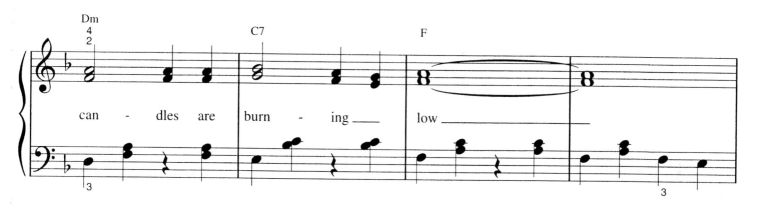

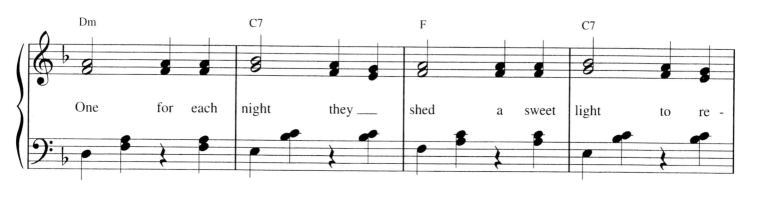

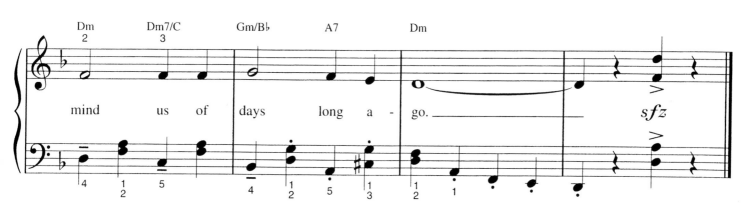

ROCK OF AGES (MA'OZ TZUR)

This is a very old song. It tells of the many times Israel struggled to be free.
It tells how the Jewish people stayed strong because they believed in God.
"Rock of Ages" is sung after the kindling of the Chanukah Lights.

TRADITIONAL
Arranged by DAVID KARP

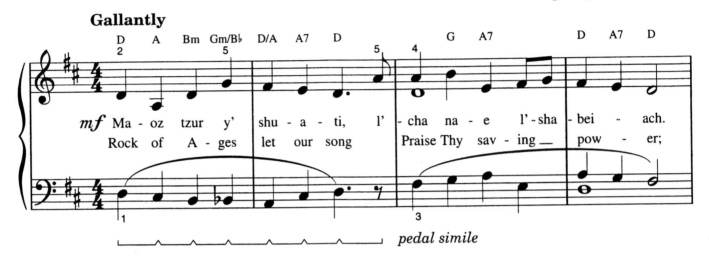

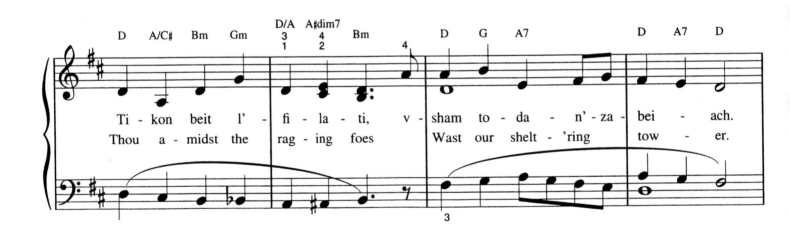

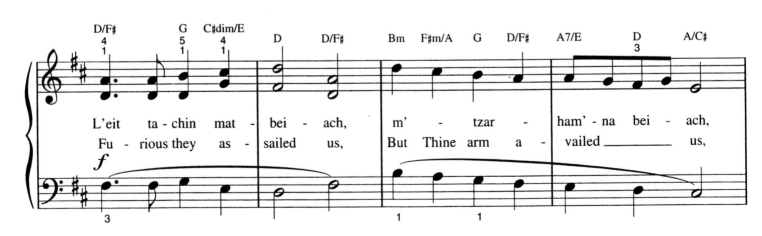

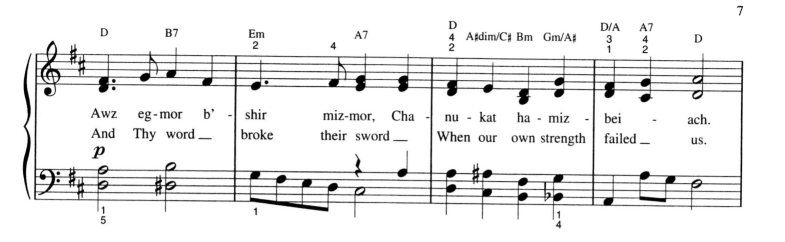

EL96112

MY DREIDEL

A dreidel is a top containing four letters, one on each of its four sides. The four letters represent the Hebrew words for "A great Miracle Happened There." Children play games with their dreidels during the eight days of Chanukah.

TRADITIONAL
Arranged by DAVID KARP

EL96112

9

EL96112

CHANUKAH

This song tells us some of the fun things that we do during Chanukah. We spin dreidels, light the menorah, and then eat potato pancakes and jelly donuts.

TRADITIONAL
Arranged by DAVID KARP

Happily, not too fast

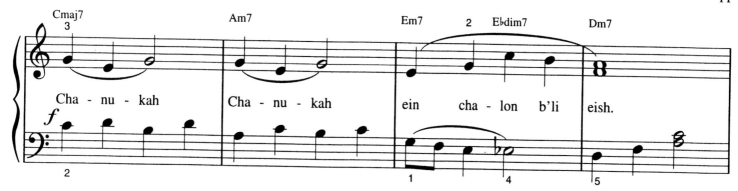

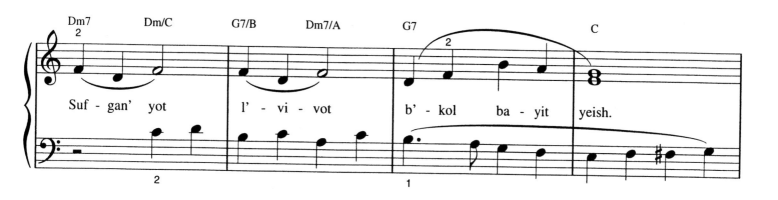

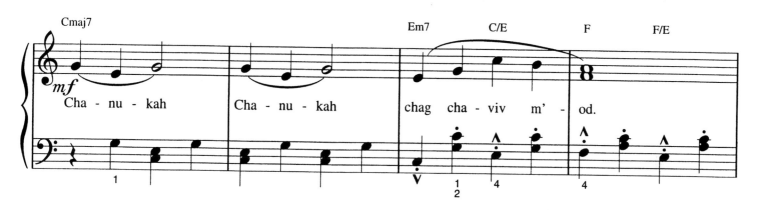

Translation:

1. Chanukah, Chanukah is such a beautiful holiday.
Lovely light all around brings joy to children.
Chanukah, Chanukah, turn, turn the dreidel.
Turn, turn, turn, turn, turn, turn,
What a pleasure and delight.

2. Chanukah, Chanukah, no window is without light.
Donuts and latkes are served in every home.
Chanukah, Chanukah is a very lovely holiday.
Sing out, sing out, rush to dance.

EL96112

Passover

The Passover story is found in the Book of Exodus in the Hebrew Bible. It is a story about freedom, God, a man called Moses, and the Jewish people. With God's help, Moses frees the Israelite people from their slavery in Egypt.

Some of the Passover symbols and rituals are the *seder* meal, the *Haggadah* that tells the story, and *Matzoh,* the flat bread eaten by Jews during the eight days of Passover.

Dayeinu

Eliyahu Hanavi

Chad Gadya

EILIYAHU HANAVI

Elijah is a prophet of hope and peace. Welcoming his presence is an important part of the Passover seder.

TRADITIONAL
Arranged by DAVID KARP

Moderato

Translation:
Elijah the prophet, Elijah the Tishbite, Elijah of Gilead,
Soon, in our days, Elijah will come with the Messiah, the son of David.

EL96112

DAYEINU

Optional duet accompaniment

When used as a duet, primo plays one octave higher than written (both hands).

DAYEINU

Sung during the Passover Seder, this song tells of the many wonderful things God did for the Jewish people.
They are very grateful for all these things, saying that just one of them would have been enough.

When played as a duet, play this part with both hands one octave higher.

TRADITIONAL
Arranged by DAVID KARP

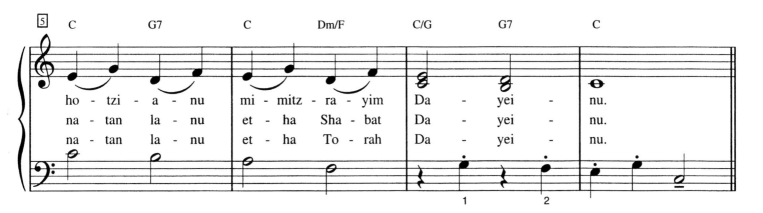

Translation:
1. Had God brought us forth from Egypt, it would have been enough.
2. Had God given us the Sabbath, it would have been enough.
3. Had God given us the Torah, it would have been enough.

EL96112

CHAD GADYA

The traditional Passover Seder ends with the poem, "Chad Gadya."
The "Kid" in the poem is a symbol of the State of Israel.

TRADITIONAL
Arranged by DAVID KARP

In a flowing manner

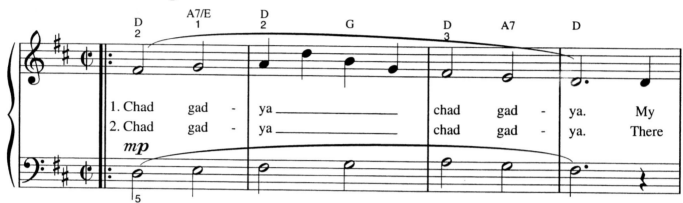

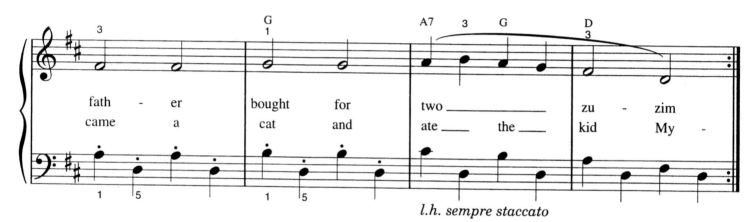

l.h. sempre staccato

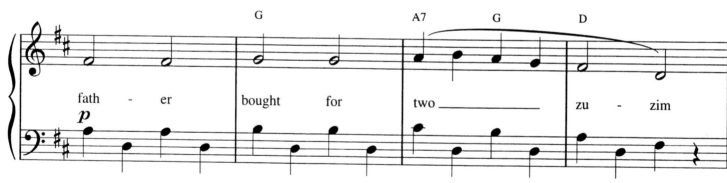

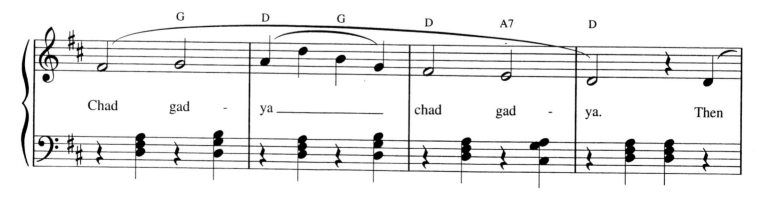

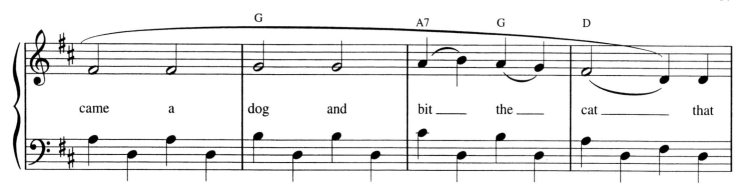

came a dog and bit____ the____ cat_____ that

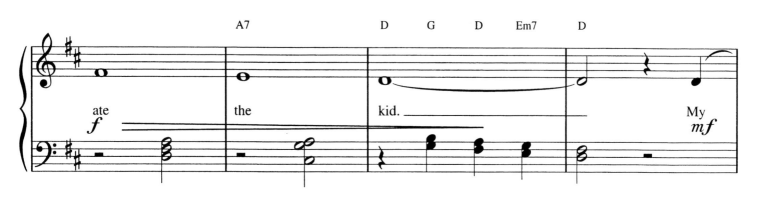

ate the kid._____ My

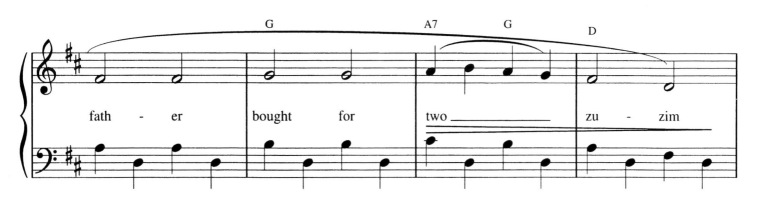

fath - er bought for two_____ zu - zim

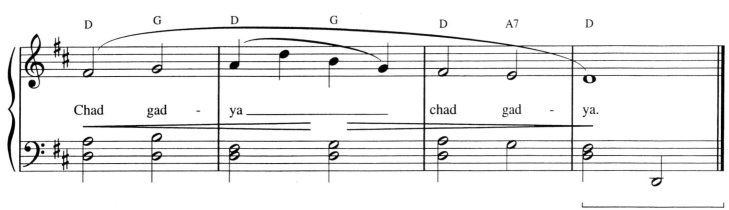

Chad gad - ya_____ chad gad - ya.

EL96112

CHAD GADYA

(see music on pages 16-17)

The following verses, which are usually half spoken and half sung,
may be adapted to the basic melodic patterns. As the song progresses, it usually
turns into a race between the young and the old to see who can finish first.

1. Chad Gadya, Chad Gadya
   My father bought for two zuzim,
   Chad Gadya, Chad Gadya.

2. There came a cat and ate the kid,
   My father bought for two zuzim,
   Chad Gadya, Chad Gadya.

3. Then came a dog and bit the cat,
   That ate the kid,
   My father bought for two zuzim,
   Chad Gadya, Chad Gadya.

4. Then came the stick and beat the dog,
   That bit the cat,
   That ate the kid,
   My father bought for two zuzim,
   Chad Gadya, Chad Gadya.

5. Then came the fire and burned the stick,
   That beat the dog,
   That bit the cat,
   That ate the kid,
   My father bought for two zuzim,
   Chad Gadya, Chad Gadya.

6. Then came the water and quenched the fire,
   That burned the stick,
   That beat the dog,
   That bit the cat,
   That ate the kid,
   My father bought for two zuzim,
   Chad Gadya, Chad Gadya.

7. Then came the ox and drank the water,
   That quenched the fire,
   That burned the stick,
   That beat the dog,
   That bit the cat,
   That ate the kid,
   My father bought for two zuzim,
   Chad Gadya, Chad Gadya.

8. Then came the butcher who killed the ox,
   That drank the water,
   That quenched the fire,
   That burned the stick,
   That beat the dog,
   That bit the cat,
   That ate the kid,
   My father bought for two zuzim,
   Chad Gadya, Chad Gadya.

9. Then came the angel of death and
   slew the butcher,
   Who killed the ox,
   That drank the water,
   That quenched the fire,
   That burned the stick,
   That beat the dog,
   That bit the cat,
   That ate the kid,
   My father bought for two zuzim,
   Chad Gadya, Chad Gadya.

10. Then came the Holy One, blest be He,
    And destroyed the angel of death,
    That slew the butcher,
    Who killed the ox,
    That drank the water,
    That quenched the fire,
    That burned the stick,
    That beat the dog,
    That bit the cat,
    That ate the kid,
    My father bought for two zuzim,
    Chad Gadya, Chad Gadya.

Purim

Purim is joyful and festive. It is a celebration of a victory over the wicked Haman and his anti-semitism.

On Purim the Jewish people retell the story in the Book of Esther (Megillah). When Haman's name is mentioned, everyone is encouraged to drown out his name by making lots of noise. The greggar (noisemaker) is used for just this purpose.

There are lots of carnivals, parties, plays and costume wearing. The food served during this holiday is Hamentashen. This is a triangle shaped pastry filled with poppyseed or fruit. This shape is symbolic of the three-cornered hat worn by Haman.

During this festival people send gifts of food to friends and give aid to the poor.

Haman, A Wicked Man

Chag Purim

Ani Purim

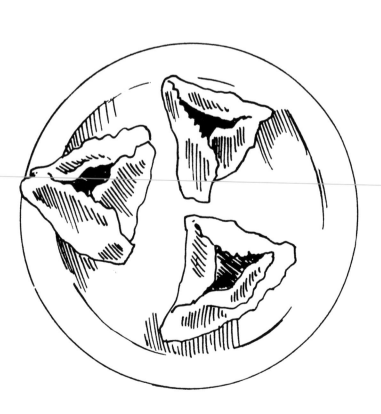

ANI PURIM
Optional duet accompaniment

When used as a duet, primo plays both hands one octave higher than written.

EL96112

ANI PURIM

This song tells about the joy of the holiday. It says, "I am Purim.
Although I visit but once a year, I am a welcome guest."

TRADITIONAL
Arranged by DAVID KARP

When played as a duet, play this part with both hands one octave higher.

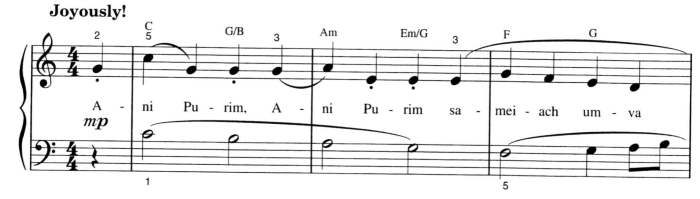

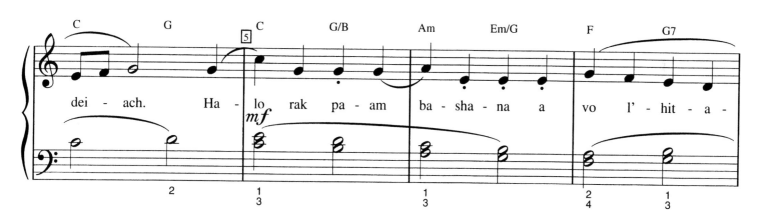

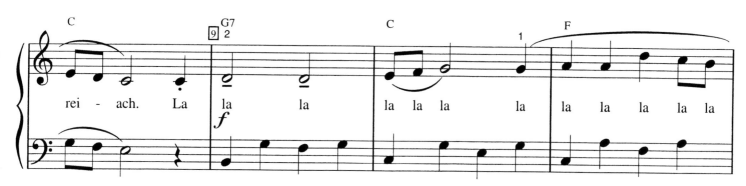

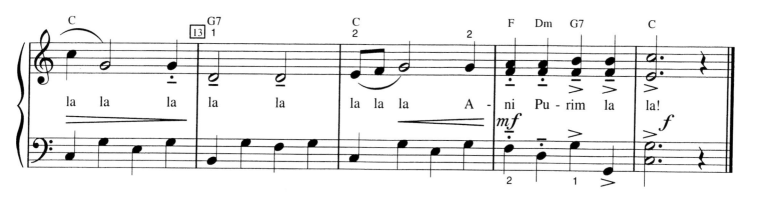

Translation: See note above

HAMAN, A WICKED MAN

When a People is saved from being hurt, merry-making takes place.
The defeat of the evil Haman is the theme of this joyful tune.

With a bounce!

Right hand *non-legato*

Arranged by DAVID KARP

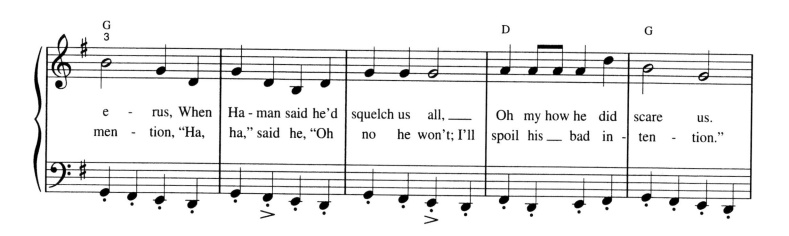

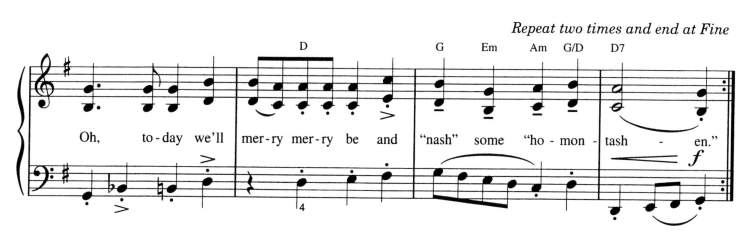

23

EL96112

CHAG PURIM

Purim is a day to be happy. An evil plot to destroy the Jews is prevented. The celebrating includes lots of merrymaking, humor and costume wearing. The noisemaker (gragger) is used to drown out the name of Haman during the reading of the Book of Esther (Magillah).

TRADITIONAL
Arranged by DAVID KARP

Translation:
Purim is a festive holiday for the Jewish people.
There are masks, noisemakers *(graggers)* songs and dances.
Let us make noise with the noisemakers *(graggers).*

EL96112

Folk Songs

The founding of the State of Israel is a wonderful and exciting story. The early settlers had a determined spirit. They worked hard at building during the day and at night they celebrated their accomplishments with song and dance. These songs tell their story.

Artza Alinu

Hatikva

Hava Nagila

Heiveinu Shalom Aleichem

Zum Gali Gali

Raisins and Almonds

ARTZA ALINU

This song tells of the early pioneers and their work in the fields.

TRADITIONAL
Arranged by DAVID KARP

When played as a duet, play this part with both hands one octave higher.

Fast and lively!

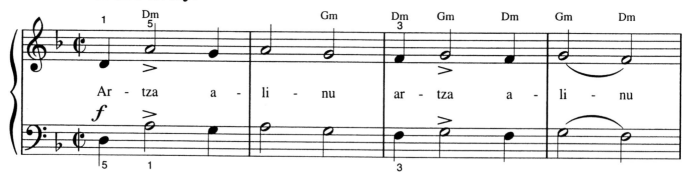

Optional duet accompaniment

When used as a duet, primo plays one octave higher (both hands).

Fast and lively!

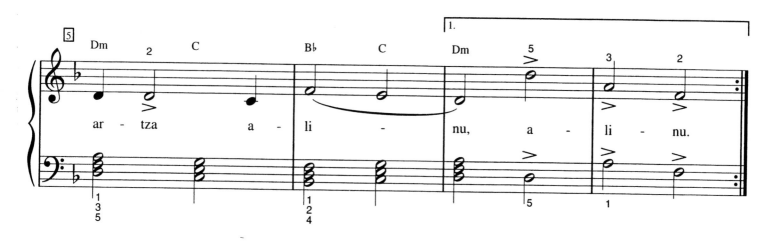

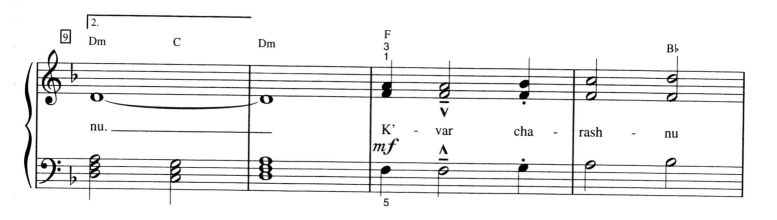

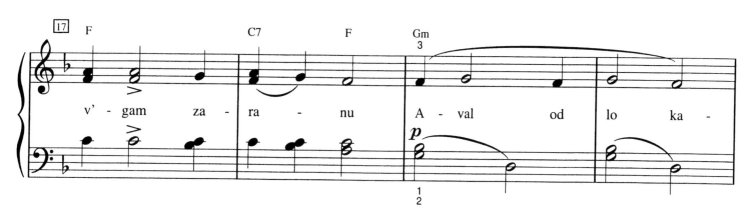

EL96112

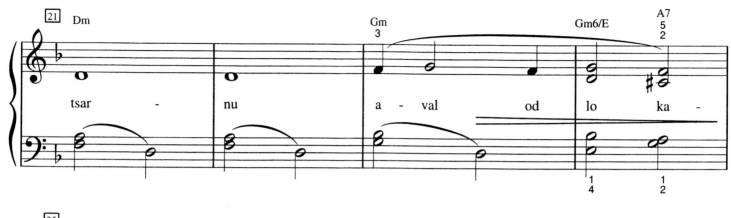

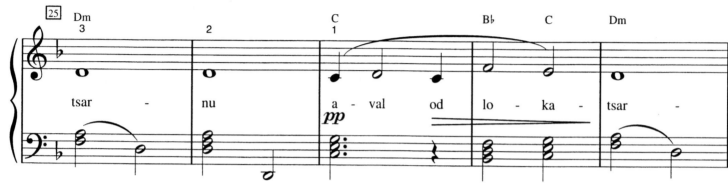

Translation:
We have come to the land of Israel.
We have already plowed and sown, but we have not yet harvested.

ZUM GALI GALI

Working on the land was the fulfillment of a dream for the pioneers of modern Israel. This song may be sung as a round. Part one begins and Part two enters when Part one reaches measure 5.

TRADITIONAL
Arranged by DAVID KARP

Allegretto

(Part one) Zum ga - li ga - li ga - li, Zum ga - li ga - li,

Zum ga - li ga - li ga - li, Zum ga - li ga - li, He - cha - lutz l' ma - an a - vo -

sempre staccato

(Part two)

da a - vo - da - l' ma - an He - cha - lutz.

Translation:
The pioneers work the land.

This accompaniment pattern may be played when this piece is sung as a round.

Gm   Cm   Gm   Cm   Gm

EL96112

HATIKVA (THE HOPE)

In 1897 the poem "Hatikva" by Natali Herz Imber became the Zionist
National Anthem. It is now the national anthem of the State of Israel.

TRADITIONAL
Arranged by DAVID KARP

Andante con moto

EL96112

Translation:
So long as still within the inmost heart a Jewish spirit sings,
So long as the eye looks eastward, gazing toward Zion, our hope is not lost —
that hope of two thousand years, to be a free people in our land,
the land of Zion and Jerusalem.

HAVA NAGILA

*Happy occasions call for singing and dancing. This
spirited song is one of the most popular folk songs.*

TRADITIONAL
Arranged by DAVID KARP

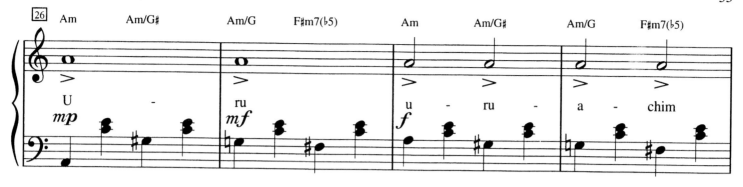

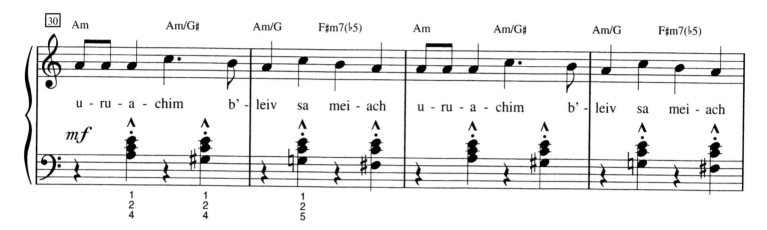

Translation:
Come let us rejoice and be glad.
Let us shout for joy and be glad.
Awake, brothers and sisters,
arise with a joyful heart!

RAISINS AND ALMONDS

(Rozinkes mit Mandlen)

This beautiful Yiddish lullaby speaks of the simple things in life: raisins,
almonds and honey. Yiddish is a language spoken by many Jews of Europe.

ABRAHAM GOLDFADEN
Arranged by DAVID KARP

Slowly and tenderly

Translation:
In the evening shadows of the ancient synagogue the widowed Daughter of Zion sits alone.
Gently she rocks her only child, Yidele, as she sings him a lullaby.
Under Yidele's crib stands a white billygoat.
The goat went away (to market) and brought back raisins, almonds and honey.
Sleep, Yidele, sleep.

HEIVEINU SHALOM ALEICHEM

*Shalom in Hebrew may be translated as **hello** or **goodbye**, and most importantly, **peace**. This short song is a song of welcome. The words mean Peace unto you.*

TRADITIONAL
Arranged by DAVID KARP

Repeat with right hand one octave higher than written.

With enthusiasm

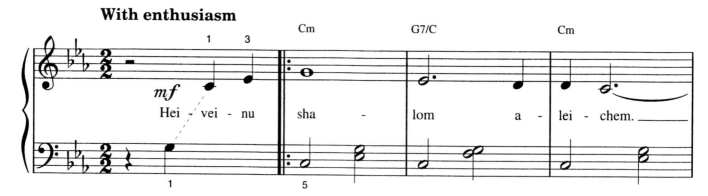

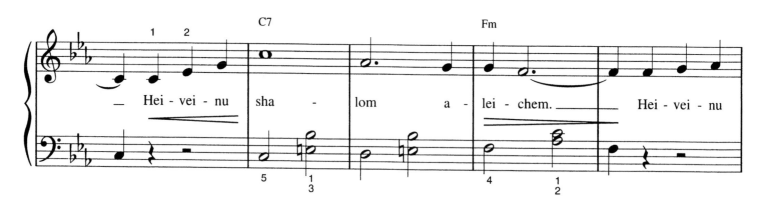

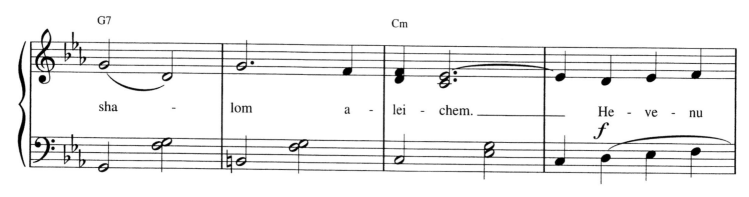

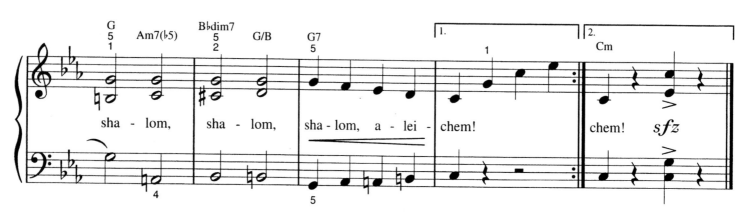

Liturgical Songs

Music has been part of the Jewish worship from its very beginnings. Jewish Liturgical music tells the history and changing circumstances of the Jewish people.

While in the ancient world, instruments were used to accompany the singing, the human voice and chanted melody has been the only music in the synagogue since the second century.

During the twentieth century, the use of instruments has returned to many synagogue services.

Liturgical music adds beauty and enjoyment to synagogue prayer and times of celebration.

Adon Olam

Hinei Ma Tov

Ein Keiloheinu

Ose Shalom

Sh'ma Yisraeil

Shalom Aleichem

©OG 1990

ADON OLAM

This is perhaps the best known of all Jewish songs. For the past 600 years it has been included in the prayerbook. Because of its popularity, there are many melodies. This is one of the favorites.

TRADITIONAL
Arranged by DAVID KARP

With tender joy

A - don O - lam a sher ma - lach B' -
Ve - hu e - chad ve - ein shei - ni le -

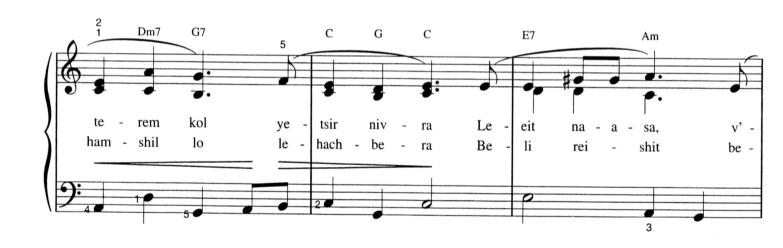

te - rem kol ye - tsir niv - ra Le - eit na - a - sa, v' -
ham - shil lo le - hach - be - ra Be - li rei - shit be -

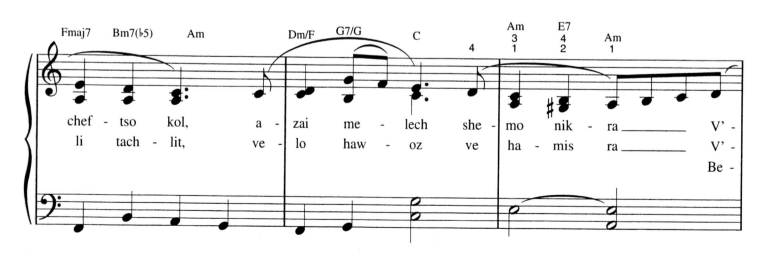

chef - tso kol, a - zai me - lech she - mo nik - ra_____ V' -
li tach - lit, ve - lo haw - oz ve ha - mis ra_____ V' -
Be -

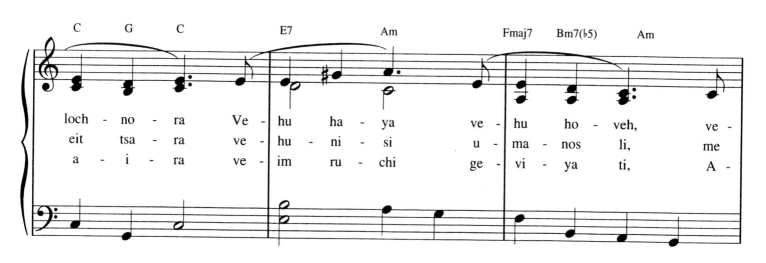

Translation:
God is the eternal Lord who ruled before anything was created.
At that time when all was made by God's will, God was called ruler.
And at that end, when all shall cease to be, God alone shall still be King.
God was, God is, and God shall be in glorious eternity.
God is one and there is no other to compare to God or to place beside God.
God is without beginning, without end. All power and rule belong to God.
God is my living redeemer, my stronghold in times of trouble.
God is my guide and refuge, my share of joy in the day I call.
To God I entrust my spirit when I sleep and when I wake.
As long as my soul is within my body, God is with me and I am not afraid.

HINEI MA TOV

The concept of brotherly love is a very important one for the Jewish people. This song comes from Psalm 133.

TRADITIONAL
Arranged by DAVID KARP

Translation:
Behold how good and pleasant it is for brothers (friends) to dwell together.

HINEI MA TOV (Round)

This folk tune may be sung as a round. Part 1 begins and Part 2 enters from the beginning when Part 1 reaches measure 9. The following arrangement provides a useful accompaniment.

TRADITIONAL
Arranged by DAVID KARP

EL96112

EIN KEILOHEINU

"Ein Keiloheinu" is a popular song that is sometimes used for the closing of the Sabbath Service. It was composed around the eighth century.

TRADITIONAL
Arranged by DAVID KARP

Joyously

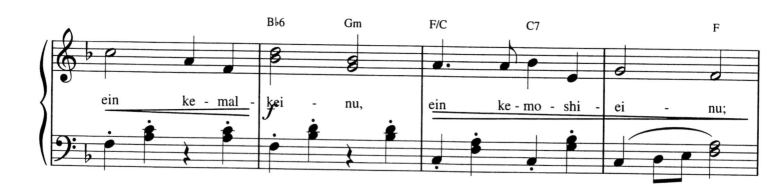

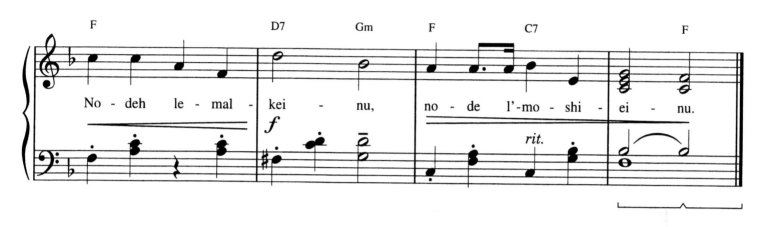

Additional words:
Ba-ruch E-lo-hei-nu, ba-ruch A-do-nei-nu
ba-ruch Mal-kei-nu, ba-ruch Mo-shi-ei-nu
A-ta hu E-lo-hei-nu, a-ta hu A-do-nei-nu
A-ta hu Mal-kei-nu, a-ta hu Mo-shi-ei-nu.

Translation:
There is none like our God; there is none like our Lord;
there is none like our King; there is none like our Savior.

Who is like our God? Who is like our Lord?
Who is like our King? Who is like our Savior?

We will give thanks to God; we will give thanks to our Lord;
we will give thanks to our King; we will give thanks to our Savior.

Blessed is our God; blessed is our Lord;
blessed is our King; blessed is our Savior.

You are our God; you are our Lord;
you are our King; you are our Savior.

OSE SHALOM

*This prayer for peace is found at the end of both the grace after meals (Birkat Hamazon)
and Kaddish. Prayers for peace are an important part of the Jewish worship experience.*

TRADITIONAL
Arranged by DAVID KARP

EL96112

Translation:
Ose Shalom (Prayer for Peace)
May the one who makes peace in the heavens
Make peace for us and for all Israel
And let us say, Amen.

EL96112

SHALOM ALEICHEM

This poem about angels was written many, many years ago. It is sung by Jews on Sabbath evening.

Melody by I. GOLDFARB
Arranged by DAVID KARP

Moderato

Translation:
Peace be to you, O ministering angels, messengers of the Most High,
the Supreme King of kings, the Holy One, blessed is He.
Enter in Peace, O messengers of peace, messengers of the Most High.
the Supreme King of kings, the Holy One, blessed is He.
Bless me with peace, O messengers of peace, messengers of the Most High.
the Supreme King of kings, the Holy One, blessed is He.

EL96112

SH'MA YISRAEIL

*Often called the "watchword of our faith" by Jews, the Shema
is an important part of the Jewish Worship Service.*

TRADITIONAL
Arranged by DAVID KARP

Maestoso, ma cantando

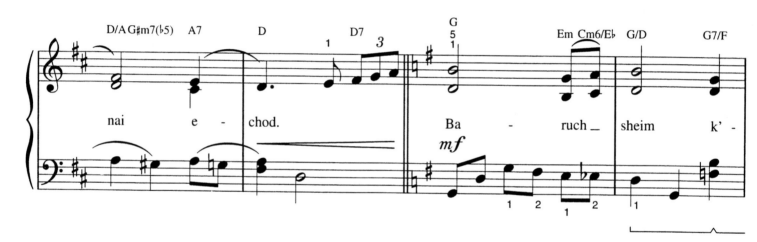

Translation:
Hear, O Israel: The Lord is our God, the Lord is One!
Blessed is His glorious kingdom forever and ever.